Senior Editor: Gwen Ellis
Creative Director: Patricia Matthews
Project Editor: Pat Matuszak
Photography: Photographic Concepts
Design: Chris Gannon

Printed in China

99 00 01 02 /HK/ 5 4 3 2 1

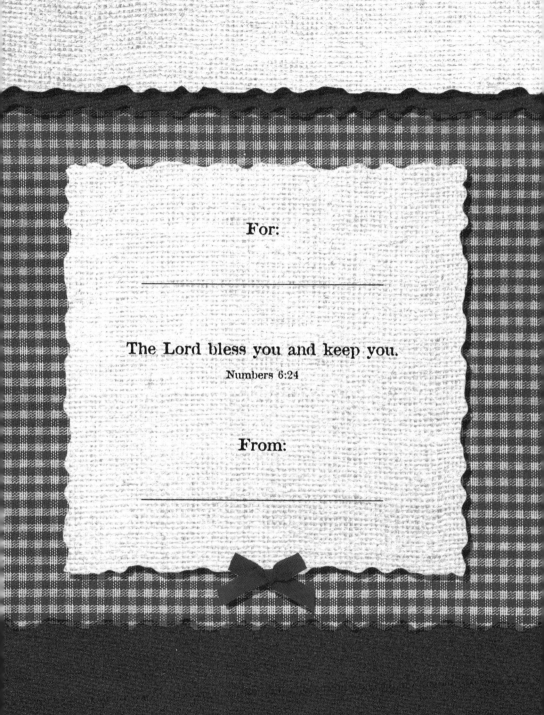

For:

_____

The Lord bless you and keep you.

Numbers 6:24

From:

_____

Love one another deeply from the heart.

1 PETER 1:22

In our friendship, God seems to weave
together all the unique threads of our
personalities— bright, quiet, coarse or
fine— until we find we have been
stitched into that beautiful coat of
many colors and textures called love.

I thank my God every time
I remember you…
It is right for me to feel
this way about all of you,
since I have you in my heart;…
you share in God's grace with me.

PHILIPPIANS 1:3, 7

All around us are friends
who seem to grow together
as garden flowers. Each gives
off its own unique scent and
adds its own special color
to the memory of spring,
summer, and fall of each
new year together.

God has shown kindness by giving you
rain from heaven and crops in their
seasons; he provides you with plenty
of food and fills your hearts with joy.

ACTS 14:17

*As sunshine and rain bless gardens
with flowers, so friendship blesses our
lives to open blooms of love, peace,
and hope. In friendship we find a
garden of color and fragrance we
have planted, yet we continue to
discover its joys as though
we'd never seen it before.*

*My heart leaps with joy and I will
give thanks to the LORD in song.*

PSALM 28:7

Two hearts that share laughter and pain.
Two souls that share a faith.
Two minds that help each other grow.
I'm glad God made us friends.

CONOVER SWOFFORD

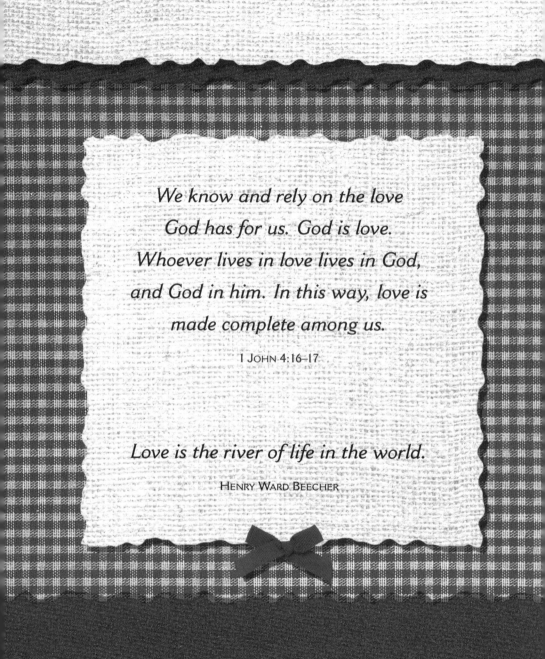

We know and rely on the love
God has for us. God is love.
Whoever lives in love lives in God,
and God in him. In this way, love is
made complete among us.

1 JOHN 4:16–17

Love is the river of life in the world.

HENRY WARD BEECHER

What is a friend? A single soul
dwelling in two bodies.

ARISTOTLE

Friendship doubles your joys, and
divides your sorrows.

ANONYMOUS

I count myself in nothing else so
happy, as in a soul remembering
my good friends.

WILLIAM SHAKESPEARE

Your friendship means so much to me—no one else can see me and my life as you do. Your understanding and thoughtfulness have helped me see myself and remember to be as patient as you have always been with me.

A friend loves at all times.

PROVERBS 17:17

Conversation.
What is it? A mystery!
It's the art of never seeming
bored, of touching everything
with interest, of pleasing with
trifles, of being fascinating with
nothing at all. How do we
define this lively darting about
with words, of hitting them
back and forth, this sort of
brief smile of ideas which
should be conversation?

GUY DE MAUPASSANT

Let your
gentleness be
evident to all.
The Lord is near.

PHILIPPIANS 4:5

*How important one life is.
One person can make such
a difference… There is something
very powerful about having someone
believing in you, someone giving you
another chance… If the whole purpose
of our lives is to become more like
Christ, and I believe it is, then we need
real soul friendships in that process.*

SHEILA WALSH

Love is the only gold.

ALFRED LORD TENNYSON

Two are better than one,
because they have a good
return for their work:
If one falls down,
his friend can help him up.

ECCLESIASTES 4:9–10

Those who love deeply never grow old;
they may die of old age,
but they die young.

BENJAMIN FRANKLIN

Carry each other's burdens, and in this way
you will fulfill the law of Christ.

GALATIANS 6:2

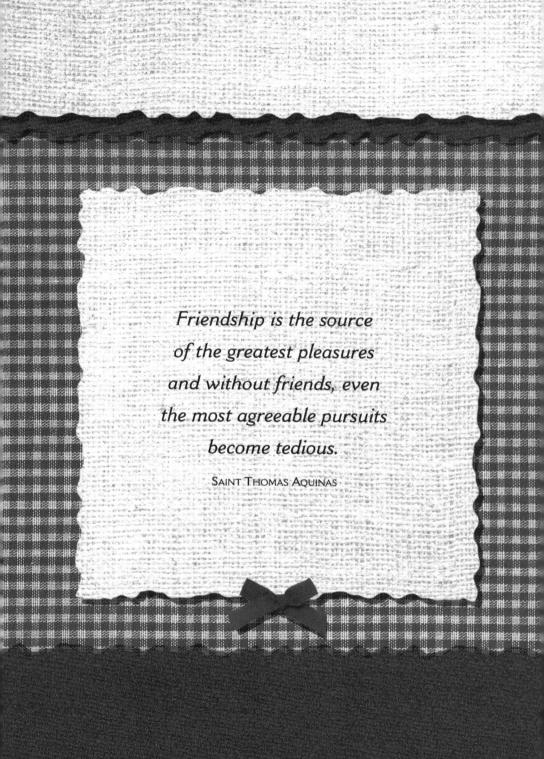

Friendship is the source
of the greatest pleasures
and without friends, even
the most agreeable pursuits
become tedious.

SAINT THOMAS AQUINAS

Friendship is one of life's best
treasures—to hope the best for someone
and know that wish is returned.
May each day bring such blessing
to my friend's life as our friendship
has brought to mine.

Most of us miss out on life's big prizes:
the Pulitzers, the Heismans, the Oscars.
But we're all eligible for a pat on the back,
a kiss on the cheek, a thumbs up sign!
Each of us has an arm with which to
hold another person. Each of us can
pull another shoulder under ours—
invite someone in need to nestle
next to our heart.

BARBARA JOHNSON

Your love has given me great
joy and encouragement.

PHILEMON 7

To love another person is to see the face of God.

VICTOR HUGO

We love because he first loved us…
Anyone who does not love his brother,
whom he has seen, cannot love God,
whom he has not seen. And he has
given us this command: Whoever loves
God must also love his brother.

1 John 4:19–21

Thanks be to God, who always leads us
in triumphal procession in Christ and
through us spreads everywhere the
fragrance of the knowledge of him.

2 Corinthians 2:14

Praise be to the God and Father
of our Lord Jesus Christ, who has
blessed us in the heavenly realms
with every spiritual blessing in Christ.
For he chose us in him before the
creation of the world to be holy
and blameless in his sight.

EPHESIANS 1:3–4

My friend, I want your life to be as
beautiful as it was in the mind of God
when he first thought of you.

CONOVER SWOFFORD

*Love means the body, the soul,
the life, the entire being.
We feel love as we feel the warmth of
our blood. We breathe love as we
breathe air, we hold it in ourselves as
we hold our thoughts.*

GUY DE MAUPASSANT

*As we have opportunity, let us do
good to all people, especially to those
who belong to the family of believers.*

GALATIANS 6:10

Some make the
world a better
place just by
being in it.

ANONYMOUS

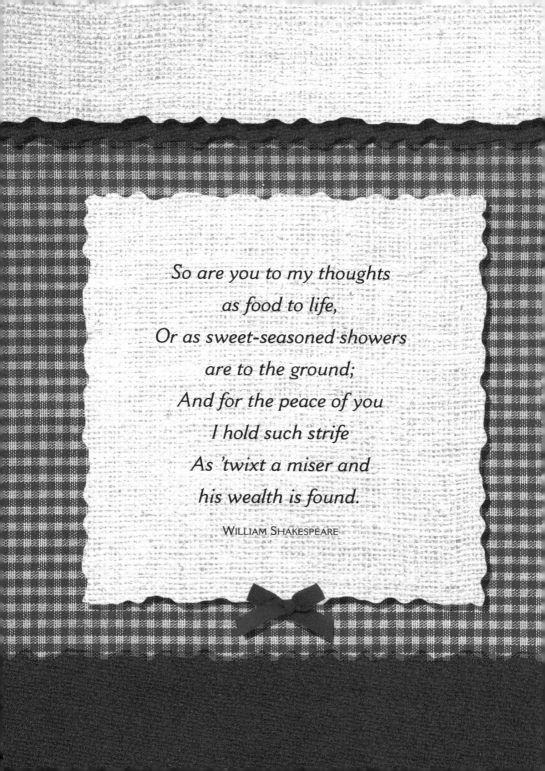

So are you to my thoughts
as food to life,
Or as sweet-seasoned showers
are to the ground;
And for the peace of you
I hold such strife
As 'twixt a miser and
his wealth is found.

WILLIAM SHAKESPEARE

Sometimes I miss hearing your voice tell that same story you've told me before—just to hear it told the certain way you tell it and to delight in the inside secret that we both know the ending together before you say it.

Perfume and incense bring joy to the heart, and the pleasantness of one's friend springs from his earnest counsel.

PROVERBS 27:9

*God will meet all your needs according to
his glorious riches in Christ Jesus.*

Philippians 4:19

*Love always protects, always trusts,
always hopes, always perseveres.
Love never fails.*

1 Corinthians 13:7–8

*When I needed a friend, God answered
my prayers and sent you to me.
The greatest gift from God
is a true friend like you.*

Conover Swofford

Therefore, as God's chosen people,

holy and dearly loved,

clothe yourselves with

compassion, kindness, humility,

gentleness and patience.

Colossians 3:12

Bear with each other.

COLOSSIANS 3:13

*There is a time for everything,
and a season for every activity
under heaven:… God has made
everything beautiful in its time.*

ECCLESIASTES 3:1,11

*Thank you for sharing the
seasons of my life, for being
there when I needed to hear
God's love in the comfort
of a friend's voice.*

*God has given us his very precious
blessing—that of true friendship.
Even when we are apart across great
distances or amounts of time, that gift
never fades and we remember the
times we shared together.*

*Above all, love each other deeply, because
love covers over a multitude of sins…
Each one should use whatever gift he has
received to serve others, faithfully adminis-
tering God's grace in its various forms.*

1 Peter 4:8–10

A friend is someone to whom you can talk forever and still find things to say, but who doesn't always need words to know how you feel.

CONOVER SWOFFORD

*One word frees us of all the
weight and pain of life;
that word is love.*

<small>SOPHOCLES</small>

*Praise be to the God and Father
of our Lord Jesus Christ, the
Father of compassion and the
God of all comfort.*

<small>2 CORINTHIANS 1:3</small>

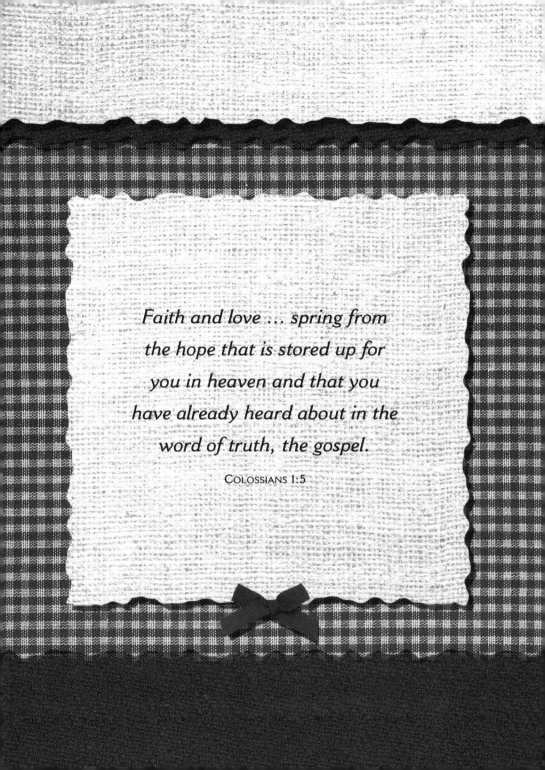

Faith and love ... spring from the hope that is stored up for you in heaven and that you have already heard about in the word of truth, the gospel.

Colossians 1:5